WITHDRAWN

FIGURE FOR SCAMANDER

AND OTHERS

ams press
new york

FIGURE FOR SCAMANDER

AND OTHERS

CAROL JOHNSON

THE NEW POETRY SERIES

Alan Swallow, *Denver*

PS
3560
O373
F5
1975

Library of Congress Cataloging in Publication Data

Johnson, Carol.
    Figure for scamander: and others.

    Reprint of the 1964 ed. published by A. Swallow, Denver,
in series: The New poetry series.
    I. Title.
[PS3560.0373F5   1975]   811'.5'4   73-179828
ISBN 0-404-56028-8
      0-404-56000-8 (SET)

The New Poetry Series

Reprinted by arrangement with
The Swallow Press Inc.
Copyright © 1964 by Carol Johnson
First AMS edition published in 1975
AMS Press Inc. 56 E. 13th St.
New York, N.Y. 10003

Manufactured in the USA

DEDICATION

In memory of Thomas Carter 1933-1963

ACKNOWLEDGMENTS

Some of these poems have appeared in *Sewanee Review*, *Poetry* (Chicago), *Commonweal*, *Hudson Review*, *Current* (Harvard), *Spectator* (London), *Abroad*, and in a pamphlet of the same title published by Thomas Carter at Martinsville, Virginia.

CONTENTS

FIGURE FOR SCAMANDER

Sorrow's springs are the same—Hopkins

It is not I who write from buried Troy,
the wine-dark sea irruptive. Sifting dirt
nine-times inters the unexploited boy,
the god his father's falling parallel, girt
with outcry from the walls, with seemly grief.
The dogs of hell have held us each at bay.
Identity no longer schools belief,
substantial as the shadow is which prays.
This was the spring our better selves betray
circle and circle till the meager sum
becomes the cipher worms enact in clay
friend unto friend. The flesh is partisan.
Only the will can use us to begin
the ancient contradiction from within.

FOR A CLASSMATE PRESUMED INJURED
IN A PLANE CRASH,
FEAST OF THE ASSUMPTION

I think it must be you fell from the sky,
pedantic child, your chubby fairness burned,
the eighteen pages of your paper gone, Burke's
Coriolanus detruded by fierce fogs
biting into Nantucket soil and scrub
with twenty-three about you slain, not fair,
or critical to see what fire might bring
from bellying darkness. Outward, at sea,
no walking fastened waters for this feast:
Our Lady treading air, by the way as you came,
Sir Thomas Hoby's, as the heavens fayre.
The army had no wars to assuage your youth.
Now terrors bless you, boy — and your lost books.
Who is wonn with a world of despayre will excuse
    these conceits
for a durable fyre in the mind.
                            ' This is a prayer,
good sir, that you come, never ould, through this
    harsh Nothing
by her gate, by her grace.

FROM A BOOK OF HOURS

A lumpish Virgin in a cloud
of muffled angels rides
on gold: the praising crowd

are deaths we might have died
denying grace for grace
the insubstantial tide

absence of time will efface
or lauds and matins prime
the hours' annealing pace.

Here spiky halos mime
the presences of love,
the stasis of that climb

in green and cobalt mov-
ing on hypostatic red.
The lines our eyes remove

in these clear colors' stead
are tensile filaments
to seem us parented,

kept home from all offence,
or married like this bride:
enceinte, indifferent.

THE VIRGIN, FOR CONTEMPLATION

This room the image of holds day, my soul,
wears him like John within Elizabeth
enleavenable dark, whose sudden toll
were water's tongues to undo clever death
as it rejoiced the Lamb we tell whose name,
whom thus the bride wore to the ready west:
fruit of the dove, act of, elliptic flame.
Our motionable mother, disarrest
the will's beloved mountain, burning door;
free us the wedding guest before desire
gives us the world outside our metaphor.
Who is our way and wise occasion, sire
in us sight. Like Mary the concentric boy,
unlock the prophet and recover Troy.

SONNET

Let us forget the horn's end of the year,
Orion marching inconclusively;
out-heroded of individual fear,
recall Odysseus apprised of Circe,
a name that burns. O Christ, we who relied
on quiet heaven and revengeless water
shall, like the friend of Dante, have descried
a strand unknown to Virgil, naked water
as salt upon our exile as the world.
(Turn backward, Alice. Is the Queen in tears?)
The mirrored senses separately curled
cannot reverse the circumscriptive years.
How should the will we fail abstractly win
sevens of light for us except for sin?

THE LOOKING GLASS

We have not lured the bird of Pentecost
into the sanctuary's thickening air.
If it were prayer by which our dreams are crossed,
we have not stirred to the resemblance there
of fire to win us comfort, or of wind,
or mother Thames to teach us whom we love,
Teresa speaking. Clearly we have sinned.
The rock we came from, father of remove,
and worlds of passion, schools me to desire
only the dark I am not, to repose
in solitude I cannot hold entire
nor move within. The likeness Alice chose
persuades me in my choosing and I wear
the Queen's passivity until I care.

The glass interprets; here we are immured.
The past has happened as if once again
we had foreknown our purging and endured,
predicting with too human cries our pain.
Wisdom is much, but always further on,
nor quite the same as its preamble spelled.
Alice at the eighth square, no longer pawn,
presumed the dream the sleeping queens beheld,
the party ending madly. In this game
the King will enter when we disappear,
though images are only things in name
and answer reasonably when we fear
to play alone. Sweet friend, opponent, shake
the shadow of my figure till I wake.

COLLOQUY FOR RUFUS JONES, QUAKER

So run as to obtain the prize—S. Paul

There is no end of running; we condone
a gospel smashed by runners after Christ.
The prize we share is blood we danced upon,
evangelled in the race of Simon-Christ.
What springing trip shall thrive us on our way
when doom divides the martyr Peter's sheep?
what blather of liturgy protect our anxious clay
lest wheat and wine conceal a realer sleep
than we have prayed for in obtaining him
morning and morning? We have run on water
colder than death; our grief is wafer-thin.
Will Quakers pray us from the impending
    slaughter —
deep after deep of cauling quiet tell
the peaceful Friends that love is where we fell?

EASTER AS LENT

He shall judge the nations, He shall heap up bodies,
He shall crush heads far and wide through the land.

Sleep that cannot forget, the indifferent dead,
even Elpenor's island-waiting can
dream leaping beasts like legend overhead.
Seas fled where once the agile Sailor ran
casting for men. Shall it begin again,
both law and portent prove the lion's tooth,
with winning smiles wind friendship up again?
 (See, it will try to take your hand.) The truth
Sappho could bring to terms; to each instead
earth, air and water's clasp will reconcile
inclusive life, the drifts of piteous dead
ascend like swimmers fishing Christ beguiles.
The Lamb's demeanor in our day is wrath
whose ruin spells our waking cenotaph.

Let mother seem to catch us; we are falling.
Mornings and afternoons have given way.
Wilder and colder than our love, they ring
the bells of Easter, mother, and they pray
Apollo's world was never blown apart.
(I ponder on a scene with children bringing
armfuls of windflowers from nowhere.) My heart,
the bells that ring the risen do not ring
the Walker back to waters where I drown,
choking on wisdom, our unleavened end.
The days of Easter wear away the crown
Christ hung for by our shreds of flesh and bend
our image for the frozen lake to catch.
My Virgin mother leaves me to my match.

16

FEAST OF STEPHEN

Thames, mortal hubris beggars us. Once more
Christ God at Stephen's side is asking blood.
Who shall outface the fierce Child and restore
the right hand of our darkness from this flood?
Stephen is our red-coated Christ to gloze
rash death with death's impermanent sacrifice.
No child of its pretended mother knows
where it will end. The breath of God is ice;
ice overwhelms the bloodstream. Our repose
is like the rotting snowman's. At this Mass,
Saint Stephen martyr, your forgiveness froze
the cocytus within our limbs like glass.
It is the dead of winter and undone
by subtle darkness the unbloody Sun.

FIGURE FOR PRAYER

Our vision is a sleep, a stir, wedding
us to the night our senses hear
beyond their kingdom where a child (soft king)
all wound with light, the fisher of our fear,
meeks us to him fiercely. Dear majesty,
lowly among the lowing beasts, a star
to find you out, let such diminish me
that wakes us to the dreams our concepts are.
The night we keep is vulnerable as thought;
our love would perish us with fiery weather,
the far-felicity our faith has caught,
were we not oned — wild charity — together.
For all the praise our minds by night could knit
would die by dark unless you kindled it.

NEW YEAR: REFLECTIONS FOR A
GAME OF WORDS

The Child is circumcised. A week of life
ripens the cry within his ageing throat.
Aslant my secular wall the Virgin-wife,
pale in her gilded pose, has it by rote.
It is the year. A year's ill fortune let
clear reason wear my wit to ancient shards
puzzling what loss loss upon loss may get
from too much light. When games were play, our
    words
discerpted from a gross of counters lay
imponderable fortune out. A child could read
what luck our play had brought. Tonight I pray
that the year's violence in me not breed
excessive light who have seen far too well
the sucking Infant in the lap of hell.

MORNING AT GESU

Christ's sickly gaze from the electric frame
(both red and green to entice our selfhood out)
dissects the shadows candled in his name.
The Masses buzz above him and without
a frail boy plucks the liturgy of song:
Bonum est confiteri Domino.
The teeth of beasts confess you. We prolong
the futile willdrift its excursive flow
through crumbled Sion. The cunning mustard leaf,
cruciferae, may teach us to grow taller
than all our loss upon this prospered land, chief-
est of which when sown (by wind) is smaller,
samer than our digressive senses spell.

Persephone, at planting time, left hell.

GLOSS ON A TEXT FROM THE MANSIONS

A sensible woman turned to poetry
who knew someone who saw her place in hell's
pitch-rooting pool, a consequence of prayer.
The King was in the center of that place,
which is the soul, as in the thick-leaved heart
of the palmito and Teresa said:
Here, we are free.

And those who walk in the vicinity,
no longer fools and traitors, parallel
Augustine who looked everywhere
but in. The hedgehog and the tortoise, carapaced,
convey the same. But if the King for his part
has not appeared to hear us, we must shed
the simple understanding,

swim outward into undiscursive seas.
He drowns with light who spouses you and tells
the will within this dazzle how to share
the intolerable burden of his grace.
(How few his friends are who can bear this art.)
My God the noises it makes in the head,
of brimming rivers.

So upward is the soul's velocity.
Well, it would be the end of us unless
his majesty had set us to prepare
against ourselves. Who, looking back, could face
the way again? Light falls apart.
And we must be like those who never fled
the thriving dark.

ELEGY

Brow and mouth to quiet drawn,
and body by its fierce decline
gentled, a classic passage known
to closer students tha n your own,

I should translate to act from shadow,
love, in your subsuming calm.
But nowhere in the metres' flow—
fugal and reciprocal—

are thou and I a muted two,
or musics outside metaphor
that I, beyond myself, am you:
child and brother, husbander

unthrifty in becoming one.
I hear my wishing verses fail,
concluding farness, and discern
iambic is the way they run.

VILLANELLE

If there were poems in it, we might write.
The music of division keeps us clear,
as in a dream of falling, from delight.

We wake to separation in the night.
The pulse of reason echoes in the ear.
If there were poems in it, we might write,

or any music or its close requite
the reach of reason with an ordered air,
as in a dream of falling from delight.

Once it was fancy folded us with light,
a fashion of beholding each for fair . . .
if there were poems in it we might write.

I measure out old meaning with such sleight,
thinking to hold you thus, who care less, near
as in a dream of falling from delight.

Reason's going risks all gifts in flight.
So I have run to reason, unaware
if there were poems in it. We might write,
as in a dream, of falling from delight.

NATURAL HISTORY

The names of things receive in language cause:
the weight of summer within temperate spring,
vermiculate, mimetic, surfeiting
the ground with the notation of its flaws.

In music the occasion disappears,
the page it mimics temporal as lust,
the cumulative moment in arrears.
'By meeting all our transigeance is lost.'

August: the cursive grasses parching are
précis of us, more distant, singular.
And each is fool to other—in such wise
baffling the will's late instinct to despise.

THE LOSER

Not quite sublimed in this,
the ample South that rounds
our imaged selves this year,
irregular and sere,
sir, we fall quiet. Sounds
shape the well we kiss.

Where have we come from
to keep such company
and easy innocence,
sharing the Greek pretense
of gifts, the clement sea,
dreams' propagation?

Whose child are you, made glad
by nothing you can touch
or in the mind confess?
Who thinks of love the less,
mistaken overmuch
by wars we never had?

The changeling you are fares
less well and happy than
the semblance we avoid.
That anagoge alloyed
unmans in you the man
fair copies can't repair.

Cannot your verses win
your world back into view
again until each scans?
Your grandfather, his lands,
recede like tides from you,
high now and dry within.

Kentucky, Arkansas,
the bluffs that serrulate
what the red clay retains
of density with veins
blue as today the slate
Carolina sky, see-saw

in your misprison: now
archaic, somehow trite.
There is nothing close
enough to lend repose
or pity or delight,
the states have fallen so.

Your name and passion fail.
All histories lie rife,
your speaking incompletion.
Myself as guilty con
this poem of your life:
alike unbeautiful.

PALINURUS SLEEPLESS

From the Spanish of Silvina Ocampo
nudus in ignota, Palinure, jacebis harena

The waves, the seaweed and the wings,
broken and sonorous shells,
salt and iodine, unlucky weathers,
fickle dolphins and the choirs

of tired sirens singing will
not replace you the suave lands
you loitered in with quiet walk
distancing always the low ships.

Palinurus: your shut gaze
is seaward, to pacific night
no gift of sleep. Outstretched and nude

you iterate on sand your deaths.
Distractedly as stone will grow
your nails and hair among the ivy.

CATS (after Baudelaire)

The fervent lover and austere savant,
each in accomplished season, fall for cats:
peaceable, ornamental, influent,
as chill as they as well as sedentary
friends of science and voluptuary,
looking for quiet and the steeper dark.
Funereal as Hell, whose to adopt
they were had arrogance inclined or not,
they assume, dreaming, the pose of quality
as Sphinxes sound the pitch of solitude,
seeming to doze within a stopless dream,
their fertile selves a revenance intact.
Flickers of gold advance the edge of black,
vaguely suffuse their pupils: and occúlt.

FROM THE ENVIRONS TO THE CARMINE

Ogives depending sparrows done-
in, pheasants, and a shrouded faun
posit November. The piazza fills.
Firenze, shutterless, details
the gravid fogs with birds across.
The colourist Masaccio's gloss
withindoors works residual blues
to christenings, and Peter's Jews
shiver before the folded light
while supple in our Fall: The Flight—
Dear Tom the master proving how—
Eve, Adam, and the angel flow
distinctly into sensuous care
this Jesus tempers with a stare
the tense apostles imitate
like cripples whose delays restate
falsely of grace its intervals.
In colours cumulous these walls
spell out our distance, our traducing dust.
Live pigeons rise where old relations rushed.

SPEECH AFTER DREAM

Body of our blame,
no negligible *ens*
that practice shall make tame,
I speak of your pretense,
moved as by once a kiss
malingered in to bare
a brave dimension, this
still-predicating care
whose image in restore
fakes order from rapport.

Is distance anything
our converse can make light,
or leisure, editing,
compose to eloquence?
Dear, tacit acolyte,
what warmth we did evince
does breed and bears the source
dreams tender and dare sleep
dissembling . . . not to keep
fair supposition's force.

A JOURNEY THROUGH SPAIN

Even maps of it are scarce.
After Camargue,
sliding to Barcelona,
hard by the tracks, the textures of coal fires
severally pock the way

candescence steepens toward to pass.
Mistral and Rhone:
elisions, the marine
graveyard at Sète gone east as Valéry,
fallen away before discourse.

The Pyrenees, the sea's donnée
black salt lean close,
fibers of rain, redundant
harbour, Beléns and evergreens being hawked.
At twenty the Cathedral's locked.

In mended capes the *guardia*
shiver and lounge.
The facile spitter aims.
In perfect inertia over the Prado stairwell,
falling, the unclothed youth.

He is a mime, and we are players
oppressed also,
falling by forms until
to this extent all lying forms annul
all love with nakedness,
as absence will.

OVER THE GRAVE CITIZENS OF FLORENCE, SANTA CROCE

The rigor of this gentry judges me,
whose bodies, immune echoes in relief,
erasure graces now with subtlety.

Here are the poets, and their verses lie,
a competence upon them past belief,
the rigor of this gentry judging me.

The immortal dead are livelier than we.
These are the stones that lend them afterlife.
Erasure graces them with subtlety.

The element of words, this usury,
not purchase and apprenticing enough,
the rigor of this gentry judges me.

One who is a poet cannot be,
except the passion these absenting give.
Erasure graces all with subtlety.

Absence is in the fact—preempting key
the walks in Florence lead us to receive.
Erasure graces thus with subtlety
the rigor of this gentry judging me.

SCHOLAR'S SONG

Assurance, purpose and the futile turns
of verse deride us with our lively powers.
Who is a poet that can read the loose
analogies of passion? Out of use
the definitions coercing desires.
Formless, unpurposing, the light adjourns

like-seeming shapes to nothing we may hold,
as in a figure or a pausing trance
the feel of reason leads us and we run
subtle, reckoning comparison.
Here in fantasmal aspect relevance
deals harshness round us, something to unfold.

Equivalences darken. We are bold.

VIEW FROM A BRIDGE, THE FAILURE
OF METAPHOR

Like reason's local cadences, the fugue
time strikes aloof the tired voyager,
musing upon the active Arno's thread,
in rain high yellow raging in its bed.
A bridge becomes this moving integer,
more numinous than the watcher's trance is vague.

Who would attribute similars to this rush?
Shuffled waters arch a kindled wick.
The city sucks their substance out of view.
Thought links with nothing vision summons to.
Drawn to this ebb, the thinker's derelict,
fishing for witness in mind's distant wash.

    Hearing this present river flow
    impartial through abstractión,
    I word from that suave undertow
    the poem's unstable sæculum.

A PERSONAL NOTE

Themes of discord, poor poet, nurture us,
verging upon pure reason as they do,
to culminate in texts such as assuage
not the perspectives thought intuits through.

Interpreted by passion, narrowly,
since we as one refute, as two complete
a dialogue predictably sufficient,
let us complain apart, in cold blood, free,
much travelled, and lie courteously with art.

POETICS OF SPACE

. . . Once Venice when it rained, soaking and cold,
swamping the steps the trestle crossed, one rode
an undulance of marble in that place,
Jesus in gold and the glazed water round
sluicing the eastern faces of the saints.

A stranger on the wrong train from Milan
saw it again, passing Ventimille,
by second class, in fitful French, dissolve
the fogs of one wet country and another.
La poétique de l'espace as it is called
for seven francs by the Academician . . .
the same plummeting down the Rhone with the
    mistral.

A MEDITATION

That fall was not from virtue that, aside,
chastises one's opinion of oneself.
Gratuitous disinterest, realised,
incorporates our nakedness. There is
no 'still life' but this casual half-dance,
the mind's made-up reflection of the flesh.
If the godhead whose likeness we admire
equivocates within this theatre,
are we then saved or lost as he, or each,
impersonating while our acts confer
the prejudice of knowledge upon sin,
the quarrels with our selves let science in?

IMPASSE

All poems are pretentious not our own,
and our own more so. Lest these lines atone,
contrived in rage the agent's to conceive,
sterility itself's derivative.

WHITE GODDESS: ACROPOLIS

The slack-jawed serpent and the painted lion
ape sacrifice above an absent prey.
These three are sacred and the moulded stone
palms to Apollo their active delay.
Where scattered stelai are Poseidon was—
the sun-struck maiden winning—and her tree
keeps and the cocky god relinquishes
the western pediment. The metope
Athena-Hera prefaces her Guest . . . .
Useful divisions moved the deities.
Armed Promachos contending the light west:
upset and wreckage, promises.
                                        The lees
of red wine mixed well yield a proper ink,
indelible as India. Zeus' daughter,
her helmet and pomegranate indistinct,
compelled from Phidias who could not falter,
cautions the known world by her boyish stance.
A poet is refuted by his sense.

AFTER PAUSANIAS

At Delphi by first light all interleaved,
the climb, the issue
are as a way postlogic to the mind
that excells the body's vision of its find.
Here is the theatre of the winsome god
who killed the snake in error and atoned,
himself annexing Pythia, the true
earth's answering center.

                        (And on that cleft road
fell Laius too, there under unhewn stone.)
The cut branch of the bay tree grown in Tempe
hails the comer.
Youths acted afterwards his cleansed return,
choirs of maidens singing where the fount
pours cold ecstatic verses past the shrine.
The early temple was a hutch of green.
Now roofless out of size the parian square—
in the robbed heroes' defect—is a scene
less plain at last than Greek wastelaying Greek.
Athena Forethought had a station here.
The vatic tripods multiplied and, often,
signs warranting, the woman poet spoke . . .
The cities spent so freely on Apollo,
laureling the killer and the kill.

A dragonfly skates air; like similes
two lovers lie in blankets by the path.
Their voices and the water make a throng.
The doubtful author of such lines as these
on difficult Parnassus thus divines
in a wild, steep, and natural sanctuary:
all cause, all want.

A PROSPECT OF PALACES: CRETE

Early, late and middle overrun
each other in this palace. On this throne
for a small man sat Minos, but first others,
worshipful, becoming connoisseurs . . .
Rites both to summon gods and to dismiss.
Sieved up still bright the wrought parenthesis.

Minos, whose brother Rhadamanthus built
this ruin, had his own light megarons:
islands of porches, acrobats in kilts
to somersault the bull, and for processions
the wide-eyed priestess of the double axe,
shapely, uncovered, polychrome and curled.
Stopped Knossos: gypsum slabs, a flame collapse,
pythoi and timbers into fetching surds
on a last morning, saffron, room by room.

Shadows like men afloat the artisan,
instructed by mirages, reconvenes:
blue monkeys picking crocuses, the bull,
dolphins—Achaean, all.
                                    A leveled hill
on the Messara plain, Phaistos, between
Ida and Asturisias again
ebbing untraceably into perfect weather
sketched clear across the German map, now rather
turns us intransitive to mind that course.
From a box at evening, laving: Orpheus.
Downhill, green almonds, gifts, loosen the ghost
xairete's, *epharisto*'s, drawn out
as verses like decipherings uncaught
from clay and the long justicing of dust.

AFTER CALLIMACHUS

AETION 1: AGAINST THE TELCHINES

The Telchines are dullards and mislike
the muses and my poems since I write
not kings and heroes by the thousand lines
but spit out as a child a shorter lot,
although my tens of years are not a few.
I tell the Telchines this:
Knowing only to waste your race's heart,
law-bearing Demeter yet outweighs the long . . .
Of two, Mimnermus proves a better maker—
not the Fat Girl. Rather, let the crane,
who savours pigmy blood, fly out of Egypt
for Thrace, the Massagetae shoot from afar off
the Medes. Those birds most sweet are brief.
Out with the jealous tribe!
Judge poems by art and not the Persian chain.
Nor look to me for a resounding song.
It is for Zeus to thunder.
                          When at first
I took a tablet on my knees, the god
Lycian Apollo told me: poet, feed
the victim fat as may be, but, my friend,
keep the muse slender.
                    And I say this as well:
Follow no carriage-way, not others' tracks.
Drive the unworn although the course is narrow.
We shrill for those who love the cicala
and not the ass's racket. Let those bray
the long-eared beast, but I would rather wings,
freely sustained upon the godly air.

42

Age fall from me (but nemesis) that weighs
like the three-cornered island on Enceladus.
The muses who regard one in his youth
will not expell from friendship when he greys.

AFTER CALLIMACHUS

AETIA 3-7: THE GRACES

Neither flutes nor garlands for the Parian graces
with the first cuttings of the sacrifice.
Once Minos with the usual offering,
the airs, even at the altar, on intelligence
of his son's death Androgeos, alone paused,
doffing his garland, bade the fluting cease.
so do the Parians now. The king of Crete,
a power on the islands, stops our song
relating how the Titan's daughters, drawn
according to Eileithyia's pleasure, stand
in finery and flowing ointments, how
with anointed hands touching these elegies
that they may keep.